RAINBOWS AFTER RAINDROPS

An Anthology of poetry

by

Jacqueline Marie Pomeroy

Published by
Athersych Publishing

© Copyright 2006

The right of Jacqueline Marie Pomeroy to be
identified as the author of this work has been
asserted by her in accordance with the Copyright,
Designs and Patents Act 1988

All Rights Reserved
No reproduction, copy or transmission of this
publication may be made without written
permission. No paragraph of this publication may be
reproduced, copied or transmitted save with the
written permission or in accordance with the
provisions of the Copyright Act 1956 (as amended)

First published in June 2006

Printed by:
Proprint, 13 The Metro Centre
Welbeck Way. Woodston
Peterborough, Cambridgeshire, PE2 7UH

Dedication

This book is dedicated to my husband Derek ('Rick') always lovingly there to help, support and encourage me. Also to Heidi, my much loved Blenheim Cavalier King Charles Spaniel, my constant companion as I write, patiently waiting for her walks… She is the inspiration for at least two of the poems in this, my first poetry anthology.

Not forgetting of course, my children, grandchildren, family and friends…

Contents: 'Rainbows After Raindrops'

Rainbows After Raindrops	7
The Royal Pavilion	8
Village Near The Sea	9
Where Do Pens and Pencils go?	10
I can't stop	11
Trembling Leaves	13
Bluebell Wood	14
Sweet Youth	15
Encounter	16
Memories of Diana	18
Bullies	19
Election of a New Pope	21
Confused Childhood	23
Fitting In	24
Wartime	27
War	28
Our Feathered Friend	29
Heidi 'Cavalier'	32
Tsunami	34
My Dog and I	35
My Dolly	37
Prisoner	40
Face of Loneliness	41
Changes	42
Debt Pile	44
Memories	46
My Friend with the Rosy Glow	47
Man from the Coast	48
On Christmas Eve	49

I believe In Heaven	51
Waves	53
On a Hillside	54
Secret	55
The Sad Skylark	56
What's Heaven Like?	57
Precious Child	58
Little Star	59
Moving On	60
Ghosts and Graveyards	62
Watch Your Step!	64
The Spot	66
Decorating	68
Say Hello to Daddy	70
When Your Eyes Grow Dim	72

Rainbows After Raindrops

Rainbows after raindrops,
Pansies in a bowl,
These things awake my heart from sleep
And resurrect my soul.

Wild waves clutching at white sand,
Palms swaying in warm breeze,
Exotic flowers in sun-kissed bowers
Give my sad spirits ease.

Red, red robin on a bough,
Her breast a glowing fire,
In peaceful sleep, resolve will keep
Her from the cold quagmire.

How little we have in common –
That little bird and I!
She cannot talk; she cannot walk,
And me? I cannot fly.

The Royal Pavilion

The Royal Pavilion in its magnificence,
Stands proudly shimmering in the noon heat,
Travellers gasp at its glory and splendour,
Photographers snap from the bustling street.

Pigeons and seagulls and starlings then gather,
Painting their picture, for us, way on high,
Each species possessing a unique behaviour,
Displaying its wings in a perfect blue sky.

The magical domes with their scorched summer pinnacles
Flirt with the blooms in the gardens beyond,
Withholding their sweet charms in anticipation,
As the romantic whispering breeze drifts along.

Whilst not far away children laugh sing and play,
Building sandcastles and splashing around,
Oh, what better sounds could live up to the splendour,
Of Brighton Pavilion and glorious grounds.

If the Prince Regent could see Brighton now,
And how it has blossomed into its peak,
Such tales of delight at each wonderful sight
It would tell – oh! If it could just speak.

Village Near the Sea

In that village near the sea
Where weeping willows ne'er are still,
Nudged by breezes easily,
Whisp'ring o'er each vale and hill.

My heart yearns for bygone years
Spent so sweetly in thy gaze,
Our souls unite through veils of tears,
I seek your grave as in a daze.

No grave with headstone or with flower,
No coverlet adorned with grass;
My own beloved's sacred bier
Lies amid the coral mass.

As tempest raged in heavens then,
Parting lovers close entwined,
Oh! To feel your arms again;
Such cruelty to heart and mind.

As tempest tore you from my grasp
And as that vessel tossed you down
'Neath the waters deep and dark;
All hope was lost, the sea had won.

Now I wonder with our son,
Pointing out where you might be,
By the willows weeping still,
In that village near the sea.

Where Do Pens and Pencils go?

Just where do all the pencils go and all the pens and things?
One minute they're in front of you, the next they've sprouted wings;
You search and search in every space, but never can you find
That pen or pencil tucked away and now you're all behind.

You grow convinced that they're alive, forever teasing you,
You sigh exasperated 'now what shall I do?'
It's late at night, the shops are closed, your friends are all in bed,
You've got the urge to write those words before they leave your head.

You climb the stairs and say your prayers, then slide beneath your cover,
You drift away and cuddle close to your beloved lover;
Strange, imaginary sights will travel through your night,
Pens and pencils dance before your eyes till early light.

Ghostly apparitions, in circles racing round,
Then dawns the morning bright and clear, but still they can't be found;
Never will I understand and never will I know –
As long as I am on this earth, where pens and pencils go!

I Can't Stop!

I can't stop writing poetry,
My fingers won't keep still,
Forming rhymes within my brain,
I guess they always will.

I was not sure I had the gift,
But time and time again
I touched the paper with my pen
And there flowed each refrain.

I tried to hold it back sometimes,
But then to no avail;
My hand would move against my will,
My pen would never fail.

The rhymes they came from nowhere,
Like magic they'd flow on each line,
They'd form themselves into the words –
I needed every time.

They interrupted conversations,
And got in the way of peace,
I'd wake with ideas at 3am,
The rhyming would never cease.

I know I'll keep on writing
Until my last goodbye
And I hope they'll write an epitaph
To suit me when I die.

It doesn't matter if it rhymes,
Or if it's merely prose,
And long as the words are meaningful
And penned by someone close.

A smile will shine upon my heart
And I'll be satisfied;
I'll pray they all will wish me well
And say – at least she tried!

Trembling Leaves

The bold oak sighs,
The wind bades her tremble,
Her leaves take flight.
Is this fright
At the terrible storm
That comes in the night?
The day will dawn
With sad, bad news
Of death and blight,
Broken hearts torn
Of those who mourn.
After a while –
A deathly hush
Descends on the forest;
Not one bird sings,
Save the song thrush,
Who with reluctance
Stays her wings;
Then soft she sighs,
Just the once…
Then like the leaves –
Takes flight.

Bluebell Wood

Oh bluebell wood, your carpet so inviting
Beckons me to tread your virgin path,
Breezes gently coax your buds exciting
To flower, amid the dreadful aftermath.

Turning for a moment, my eye captures
The sorry wake my foot has dared to tread,
Pressing, crushing, cruelly destroying,
But look, and look once more, they are not dead!

They've held their heads so deftly in defiance,
Petals trembling where my feet once stood,
They'll rise together proudly in alliance
And dance within the shadows of their wood.

Sweet Youth

Casting glances o'er the roses red,
My heart thinks back, its memory intact,
To long years past, (this heart love never lacked)
That wondrous time we dreamed in nuptial bed.

And then its tuneful song the thrush began,
Its music hovered round that wooded glade,
'Neath grand and towering oaks bold shadows made,
That summer night you'd scarce become a man.

And eerie silence came when wind had died,
As songbird slumbered, not a creature stirred,
Your heart reached out with not a single word
And joined with mine that night and softly sighed.

Encounter

'Twas a lifetime ago on the brow of a hill,
On a moor where the heather grows,
I spied a dark maiden with beauty so fine,
Wearing ancient and tattered clothes.

Such a magical spirit descended on me,
But my heart became wearily sore,
The gale began whipping and biting and gripping
Her delicate frame to its core.

My voice it was silent, then just at that moment
Her flashing eyes bored into me;
I was held in my track, as I dared to glance back,
Then we kissed 'neath a moribund tree.

The rain lashing down took its toll, as the wind
Then howled, as it yelled on that hill;
My heart it was gladdened, not dampened, not saddened,
I held the frail body quite still.

She whispered so sweetly, her voice sang like church bells
But caused my soul tremulous grief;
Then she cried 'I am Jasmine, but pine not for me,
For our fleeting encounter be brief.'

Then that skeletal form made me cry out in pity
And vow to give comfort and light,
But she tore from my grip, so sudden the slip,
Then hurried into the black night.

All at once she was gone – and I all alone
Then knew that I never would find –
The like of this vision, sent from the high heaven,
Though I live to one hundred and nine.

She never did happen again on that moorland
Where heathers abundantly grow,
But if you should meet her, then hurry to greet her,
And tell her I love her so.

Memories of Diana

Sad thoughts of our Diana still wander through my brain,
'Tis many a year since she passed by, but thoughts of her remain.

I picture her with landmines and counselling the poor,
Cuddling sick babies and others at death's door.

So absolutely human, affectionate and kind,
Leaving all formality and protocol behind.

She suffered such vexations commoners don't understand,
With no one to allay her fears, or take her by the hand.

She tried in her own special way and always did her best,
But felt inadequate as if she'd failed to pass the test.

Just why was she remarkable? I guess we'll never know;
The grief of every nation told how we all loved her so.

God sends a special person only once in each lifetime,
So I've sent him endless gratitude that she was born in mine.

Bullies

Bullies are such awful types, they push and shove and hit,
Victims usually half their size – bear the brunt of it;
They gather other people in and get them on their side,
Until they end up in a gang – and spread fear far and wide.

Alone, they never are as brave as when the gang joins in,
They are such cowards deep inside; they'll really never win;
They'll never have a real true friend, this joy they'll never feel,
It's being liked just for yourself that makes a friendship real.

They pretend that they don't care and hold their heads up high;
It's never pride that leads to this,
They haven't a friend in the world to miss,
Or who cares if they live or die.

One day they may just see the light and realise their sin,
The tables may just turn on them, their victims then will win.
The weak will then become the strong and as years come and go,
The victims will remember what happened long ago.

But they won't push and shove and hit and they won't reprimand
the bullies who were cruel to them, they'll do their best to understand;
For victims usually are the types who'd hardly hurt a fly,
A kind and gentle nature will surely win through by and by.

Election of a new Pope

Christians pray around the square,
The Pontiff ails; he is not there,
A sob arises from the crowd,
For on this day tears are allowed.

The sad news breaks – our Pope is dead!
His final prayers have all been said,
The funeral takes place tomorrow,
The throng will wail with tears of sorrow.

They've kept their vigil faithfully,
Representing you and me;
Procession now will grace each street –
John Paul once trod with aged feet.

The crowds disperse with swimming eyes,
Now they've bade their last goodbye's
Wond'ring who'll be next in line,
Surely God will send a sign.

A re-election date is set,
They must prepare the red carpet,
But first the chimney must belch forth
A pure white smoke, for all its worth.

Christians pray both day and night,
Is that black smoke, or is it white?
A cheer erupts; the birds take wing;
The people's hearts rejoice and sing.

The smoke is definitely white,
Two thirds majority this night
Has now ensured our Pope is picked;
His name will be Pope Benedict.

Confused Childhood (Sea voyage, 1954)

Long ago, I sailed the foamy sea
On Atlantic waves by night and day,
To a far-off land three thousand miles away,
Memories lingering, bittersweet for me.

Is this because I'm good, or am I bad?
Such confusion in this malleable mind;
Are they being caring, or unkind?
Should I feel excitement, or be sad?

Just why were they sending me, that day,
From a warm and loving mother I adored,
Across to picturesque Canadian shore –
To stay with aunts and uncles, far away?

Wishing 'Bon Voyage,' those waving hands –
Saw I in the distance from that ship,
I with swimming eye and quivering lip,
Experiencing things that I don't understand.

Never will I know the deep down cause,
Which changed my life then, so dramatically,
Was my spirit ready to be free –
From tugging ties and ever open doors?

No answer. A titanic question lives
And troubles me and stays to haunt me now,
Leaving me to guess and wonder how
This torment-ridden soul somehow at last forgives.

Fitting In

I never felt I fitted in,
I somehow felt –'apart,'
Though others tried to welcome me
And open up my heart.

It never seemed to quite work out –
This 'fitting in' procedure,
It baffled me and wore me down,
I'd stand apart, with saddened heart,
Rejection's common leader.

I'd blend in with the background –
Feeling non-existent,
Unnoticed and forgotten,
Cold, bereft and distant.

When gathered round a table,
My opinions didn't count;
It's as though I were invisible,
Misgivings then would mount.

If I'd been loud and talkative
And spread opinions round,
I'd have those colleagues flocking,
Acquaintances door-knocking –
To enjoy my dulcet sound.

Something always held me back
And caused me endless strife;
I'd try to change my attitude
And make the best of life.

Not seeking popularity,
Or to stand out from the throng,
Just accepted and included,
Treated fairly all along.

But fairness didn't happen
And I'll never understand –
How this 'fitting in' quite works
And how these things are planned.

Self-pity I don't feel at all,
It's not reality,
In fact it's strengthened my resolve
And set my spirit free;
My pity's for the fun they missed
And the side they'll never see.

They'll never know the wonder
Of the friendships I have made,
The sounds of fun and laughter –
Such memories never fade…

So I'll just go on as I am
And hold my head up high,
Proud of my achievements
And never will I cry,
In this, the last lap of my life,
Until my last goodbye.

Most people were oblivious,
Quite missed the point you see;
They failed to open up 'blind' eyes –
And know the real, true me.

Wartime

My heart's desire would be to see
An end to war both near and far,
And I would wish upon a star -
Man would not die so needlessly.

And then to longing day by day
That homicide ne'er did exist,
Then I would add upon this list -
Cast all brutality away!

How sad and deep within each heart,
Residing fears locked tight within –
Gained stronghold as lives did begin,
Practised oft' when lives were torn apart.

Think on then of this changing world,
And pray awhile with eyes shut tight,
And once again with all your might,
Then once that peace be ours to hold.

War

Soldiers crouching on the ragged front,
Bellies dragging through the blood-soaked earth;
Terror coursing through the mother's sons –
for all it's worth.
Their veins erupting, twinned with stomach churns;
Teenagers' bodies rotting in their graves -
dug swiftly by their sobbing counterparts,
Their lives they gave.
For what? Their mothers weep and wail and cry;
The knocker's rap, death's eerie messages conveyed.
'I knew it would be mine – my baby boy!'
The mothers' anguish! –
the abandoned wife's goodbye.

Our Feathered Friend

One sunny morning we did sit, to eat our breakfast bacon,
We peered out of the window and thought we were mistaken;
A beautiful sleek blackbird stood pecking at the grass,
His feathers black and shiny, his beak as bold as brass.

He really looked quite handsome as he flew onto our gate,
But he was not alone for long, for then appeared his mate;
She was a different colour and her beak appeared more fair,
She was a lovely shade of brown. Oh! What a pretty pair.

As we sat outside on sunny days, or when digging in the ground,
He took a chance and ventured close – each day he came around.
All through summer into autumn, every day he came.
By now he looked dishevelled – we must give him a name.

'Scruffy' seemed to fit the 'bill' this name we can't forget,
We grew to love our Scruffy as if he was our pet.
Each day he'd come for raisins and he'd do a little 'trick'
First he'd tap the bedroom window, to wake both me and Rick.

He'd hop up on the garden bench, then he'd get his reward,
He knew he'd have to do this first, then off again he soared;
Each spring he'd bring his 'wife' along, they both knew we'd got food,
But it was more exciting when followed by their brood!

One day we got excited – he ate raisins from my hand,
I whispered 'Rick, oh come and look,' I knew he'd understand.
Another day when blizzards came, could not believe I saw –
him hop inside for shelter – right on the kitchen floor.

He'd hop into our kitchen, to visit like a friend,
We were so fond of Scruffy, we hoped this wouldn't end.
But we knew one day he'd fade away and go just like the rest,
So we said a prayer that he'd live long and happy in his nest.

The snowflake season soon approached and brood had long since gone,
Our Scruffy remained faithful, as winter lingered on;
And then one day we realised he'd not been for a while,
We missed our little feathered friend, he'd really made us smile.

We waited, but his visits stopped, things never were the same
Then somehow it just dawned on us – he'd had his little game
We won't forget our Scruffy, though twenty years have passed,
He must be at bird heaven's window, a-tapping on the glass.

Heidi Cavalier (Cavalier King Charles Spaniel)

She lies upon her little bed,
Dreaming dreams of being fed,
Given walks and then a treat,
The sweetest dog you'll ever meet.

Waggy tail and big brown eyes,
Mind mysterious and wise,
She only knows the kindest ways,
She's been like this for all her days.

Waiting for me at the door,
Two hours or three, or maybe four,
Therapy for when I'm blue,
Loyalty both sure and true.

I'd peered and cooe'd at each cute pup,
And one by one I'd picked them up,
Some just wriggled their way free,
Others ran away from me.

One single puppy liked me best,
She snuggled down upon my chest,
Then stared into my eyes serene,
The cutest gaze I'd ever seen.

A look of calm upon her face,
Her little nose then took its place,
She pushed it under my elbow,
This surely set my heart aglow.

I went away and tried to find
Activities to fill my mind,
Three full days passed with little food,
I realised it was no good.

She entered every waking thought,
And in my dreams she even sought –
To haunt me with her winning charm,
(Still 'felt' her nose beneath my arm)

Then just in time I made the call,
She'd been for sale to one and all!
I got there in the nick of time,
Relieved, I sighed 'at last she's mine!'

Now she lies upon her special chair,
In peaceful sleep she slumbers there,
Cute and comforting and still,
I love her and I always will.

Tsunami (26th December 2004)

Oh! The devastation on that distant far-off shore,
Who would have thought that any moment giant waves would score,
And cruel waters murder, maim and wipe away from earth
The folk relaxing by the sea, enjoying sun and mirth.

The people on their holidays, the residents there too,
Who'd never ever heard the word 'tsunami' – well have you?
It means an earthquake over there has struck the deep sea bed,
Killing children, men and women, tens of thousands now are dead.

Both rich and poor and even all the people in between,
It did not differentiate. No one could have foreseen –
The dreadful tragedy, the menace of that tidal wave,
The crying and the agony, as all their lives they gave.

Think on then as you go about your usual daily life,
How fortunate we are to be so distant from this strife,
Not so all the sad families who've lost their loved ones dear,
We pray that they might have the strength this burden so to bear.

My Dog and I

My dog and I, we love to walk and walk,
She cannot laugh or sing, she cannot talk,
But oh! The pleasure when it's her and me,
Just her and me and birds for company.

When grey skies loom and rain is lashing down,
Or in the dimness of autumn's twilight
And even in the darkest dead of night,
Her needs I must fulfil before my own.

Her pleading eyes meet mine for nature's call,
Though I'm sore and aching in my feather bed,
'Tis then I drag my migraine wounded head
To parkland, clutching grimy, battered ball.

I spy her in the distance –
Through my dim, half-vision eyes
And pray she will obey my timid cry,
Trembling with relief as she 'comes by.'

And onward as we trek our way back home
She's happy just to feel her mistress near,
I am to her the thing she holds most dear,
It matters not that we are here alone.

A crackling flame lights up her liquid eyes
Bringing comfort to my ailing heart,
She needs no word her dispatch to impart,
Then in the dancing firelight she sighs.

Fireside companion, therapeutic friend,
Soul repairer, socialising star,
To me, my faithful one, these things you are
And may you walk with me to journey's end.

My Dolly

My dolly's face was moulded
In porcelain so fine,
Her pretty eyes were bright sky blue,
Her cupid lips divine.

Her hair was real, it's silky feel
Thrilled me through and through,
Each night I carried her to bed,
I kept her as I grew.

Her clothing was best quality,
A purple hat she wore;
Her socks and shoes were purest white,
She thrilled me to the core.

She had white teeth and ruby mouth,
She had a moving tongue,
I loved her dear and each New Year
She'd join the happy throng.

She had a lacy petticoat
And pantaloons beneath,
So clean and starched and beautiful,
They matched her pure white teeth.

She kept here limbs together
With a stretchy band of rubber
Hidden in her body,
As I would soon discover.

This band was of the thickest kind
That you would ever see,
And never would it fail to hold
Its elasticity.

If any of her limbs detached
It was a daunting task
To reattach each arm or leg,
An adult I would ask.

I took my dolly everywhere
That mummy would allow,
She drew such admiration,
Oh! I wish I had her now.

What happened to my dolly?
Now that's a mystery,
She may have found another girl
To love her tenderly.

It may be fifty years ago,
Those years have long since gone,
She was mine for one brief time,
But thoughts of her live on.

One day I may discover
In a little antique shop
My dolly waiting there for me,
And my eyes will surely pop.

I'll take in lots of pennies
And my dolly I will buy,
Then we'll be re-united
And I'll keep her till I die.

Prisoner

Enveloped
In darkness
In a cold cold cellar
One sunbeam
Struggles to reach me
To cheer me…
In captivity.

Face of Loneliness

What gain have I with vast estates and land,
What good is wealth to me unless it's shared,
Better to be loved than no one cared,
Without a friend in sight where do I stand.

What if I lay crying half the night,
Without a hand to hold in my distress,
What happens when my heart craves tenderness,
When snow lay thick and bitter winds do bite.

This loneliness I find I cannot bear,
When fear crowds in and gathers in my soul
And no one loves and makes my spirit whole,
Just emptiness inside and no one there.

Changes

There's got to be some changes mum, though you're not in your prime,
You've got to get your brain in gear, you must move with the times!
We're not in 1960 mum, or even eighty four,
We've pc's, 'chips and pins' and stuff and mobiles by the score.

We're well past the Millenium, we've had the Dome and such,
Times are changing fast you know, you've got to keep in touch.
Though you've become a granny, you needn't act like one,
You know you're not bad-looking mum, when all is said and done.

It's time to look more 'trendy' mum, to look a little slick;
Here, take this cash and treat yourself, get up-to-date and quick!
That fashion turns full circle, is really very true,
It catches every one of us, including me and you.

'What's that you're saying daughter dear? I've just been into town
And what I saw within the shops – made my jaw drop down.
Is this what you call 'trendy' dear? It's really quite uncanny
That I'm now dressed in the 'latest styles' that used to suit my granny!'

Debt Pile

It's the easiest thing in the world
To take a card out of your purse
And pass it across the counter,
But it's really the start of a curse.

You will find yourself landing in trouble
If constantly buying this way;
For the goods are not your belongings
If you haven't the means to pay.

It may be a wonderful moment
When you walk from the store with your clothes,
You will feel all elated and floating
From your head to the base of your toes.

You'll rush home with joy and excitement,
Your heart will be thrilled to the core,
You'll burst through the door, worn out and footsore
And collapse in a heap on the floor.

Quite soon you will lose that excitement,
You'll be bored with the clothes that you wore;
Your feet will be itchy and roving
And find their way out through the door.

You'll arrive at the shops in the High Street
And your cards will be ready once more,
They'll jostle for space in your handbag
As they take you from store to store.

After some weeks you'll be dreading
That bill dropping through your front door,
You'll gasp with the shock that awaits you
And vow not to shop anymore.

So beware of the debts that will break you
And please don't blame the poor card;
If you end up amassing a debt-pile,
Be warned that your times will be hard!

Memories

Memories of happy days,
Though shrouded in a distant haze,
Bring to mind the many years –
We shared the laughter and the tears.

Happy hours of childhood play,
Saw us through each summer day,
Country walks and pretty flowers,
Mingled with occasional showers.

When autumn breezes rocked the trees,
We trundled through the fallen leaves,
There was not always milk and honey,
But still we laughed and found things funny.

Then the winter winds did blow,
Bringing freshly fallen snow,
And with it came cold days and nights,
And pretty scenes and snowball fights.

Then the spring did blossom fair,
And dressed the trees that were so bare,
Though seasons came and never stayed,
These memories will never fade.

My Friend With the Rosy Glow

Just where have you gone,
My friend with the rosy glow?
In her place maturity
On the face I used to know.

I'll never get her back again,
In my heart is almost pain
For the lost years,
Unshared laughter
Maybe tears.

Where are you now
My friend with the rosy glow?
Forty years have passed us by
(too long)
You're here at last
In her place.

Recognition gone
But still…
Our friendship
Lives on…

Man from the Coast

The man from the coast walked in,
There were smiles all around,
He made such an impression,
No one uttered a sound.

The man in his seaside clothes
Resembled an old-fashioned dandy,
All airs and graces and waves,
On his arm was his wife called Mandy.

He didn't utter a word,
Come to think of it, neither did she,
They made a delightful pair,
As they walked right over to me.

They still didn't utter a word,
Just as happy as happy could be,
As they stood there blissfully smiling –
They'd just got married you see.

Everyone started rejoicing,
All that is, except me,
As I tried to gain my composure,
Turning round so no one could see.

The reason the man was so smug,
It's my 'ex' here we're talking about!
The man from the coast walked in –
…and I walked out.

On Christmas Eve

On Christmas Eve I sit me down and think on days of old,
Of silent snowflakes falling, of freezing, bitter cold,
Of ladies in long dresses, a-pulling at their shawls,
Who yearn for cosy places and glowing, glimmering coals.

I think of chestnuts roasting, rich folk round fireplaces,
As sips of wine and dancing flames illuminate their faces,
Of men who pull the servant cords requesting extra logs,
Black cats, which curl up on the hearth, with Labrador type dogs.

I think on times and places, where I'd really rather be,
As I sit by my fireside, lacking company,
I hear the ring of Church bells, and singers carolling
And then I sit and ponder on what New Year will bring.

Perhaps there'll be excitement and love will come my way,
Oh yes! I'll wish with all my heart that peace be here to stay,
I'll welcome these with open arms and just a little more,
Good health with happiness thrown in and chuckles by the score.

But dears, we must not cast aside the purpose of this season,
And go about in droves to shop – oblivious to reason,
We must remember – Jesus Christ did come upon this Earth,
To save our souls from sin and justify his Holy birth.

I Believe in Heaven

I believe in heaven,
Well at least I think I do,
I've heard so many stories of it,
Surely then it's true.

I've also heard some tales
Of people having lived before,
It's jolly well intriguing,
But it could be old folklore.

There are many magical accounts
Of spirit sights and sounds,
Myself, I've never been entranced,
No evidence have found.

Is this all about believing,
Or just an inclination?
Do you need a special faith?
Or great imagination.

I've tried to find an answer
On my travels far and wide,
But I'm really none the wiser,
Oh! I wish I could decide.

Maybe I'll see an angel,
To help my faith to seal,
Or some other apparition
And then I'll know it's real.

Or hear a sound above my bed,
When the night is new,
Ah! But if I see my angel,
I'll know my life is through.

Waves

How I love to watch the ebb and flow of tides,
The shushing sounds and many more besides,
Foamy billows raining on gold sands,
Enclosing surfers' boards like giant hands.

Sunlight playing sparkly games on waves
Which lap mysteriously in and out of caves,
'Tis this which brings glad music to my ears
And momentarily allays my fears.

Waves lunging at the rough and grainy rocks,
Lapping under jetty's and through docks,
Roaring in the cruel hurricane,
Relaxing in the calmness of the wane.

And strangest pictures dance amid the foam,
Apparitions of folk long since gone,
Visiting from heaven's starry beams?
Propelling me through never-ending dreams.

On a Hillside

'Twas on a hillside long ago,
A boy and girl most fair –
Kissed the while and pledged love true,
Among the heather there.

No shelter all the long night time –
On hill with star above,
No pillow or no counterpane
To warm them in their love.

Oh! Hold me at this last farewell,
With kisses smother me!
Enchant me with thy wild, wild eyes
And I'll die for love of thee.

Secret

I hear the gentle rustle of the leaves,
The rippling stream as in and out it weaves
Among the pebbles, rocks and stones that lay
Still and silent, randomly along the way.

I wend my way with furtive glances back,
With stealth along the well-worn little track,
Well-worn, but worn down just by me alone,
To this retreat I long to call my home.
I hear the gentle cooing of a dove,
Its' sound tells me I'm closer to my love.

Another mile or so in front of me
I spy a blackbird settling in a tree;
It's been here ever since I've walked this way,
It sang as in each other's arms we lay.

He knows it's wrong to stir this love in me,
I'd die before I'd ever let him be,
I know I'll always want to be with him,
Still we both know that we could never win.

And so, this path I tread so watchfully
Now leads me to where my heart longs to be,
And though this love I am not free to give –
I'll walk this path as long as I may live.

The Sad Skylark

Sad skylark why do you mourn?
Oh! See them there, the cute new born,
Closer now, oh closer look!
Poor little souls float in the brook.

One little wing clings momentary,
Catching on the stones unwary,
Lifeless now, no fluttering wing,
Never will that sweet voice sing.

Parent cocks her little head,
Far above her babe's deathbed,
Desperate to fulfil her need,
Gaping, starving mouths to feed.

Cuckoo now in vacant nest –
Claims the space the skylark left;
Settles down to preen and rest,
Parent looking on, bereft.

What's Heaven Like?

What's in the sky mum, she said,
Heaven I said.
What's heaven mum, said she,
It's a place for you and me.

Will we have enough food, she said,
Plenty, I said.
Will we have a home, said she,
'Course we will, a mansion, see.

Will our friends be there, she said,
Eventually, I said.
Will I go to school, said she,
No need for that, said me.

What's it really like, she said,
Beyond your wildest dreams, said I,
May we go today, said she
No, not until you die, said I.

Precious Child (And Little Star)

Precious child now in my arms,
I will keep you safe from harm,
How long I've waited for this time,
Though I'm far from in my prime.

Precious child I hold you near,
Ever watchful, never fear.
I've waited patiently for you,
For years and years the longing grew
Into a vacuum deep and wide,
A yearning felt down deep inside.

With this child then I was blessed,
A little girl, she's just the best,
She is not mine, don't think it sad,
I am the mother of her dad.

This precious gift she's mine to share,
How much I love, how much the care –
Manifests itself within,
I hardly dreamed that I would win
Such affection from this child,
Soft and gentle, meek and mild.

'I love you nanny' makes my day,
All my cares just melt away,
My grandchild's love is more than gold,
This precious gift – mine, just to hold.

Little Star

Little arms that reach for me
Bring such happiness you see,
I can't resist that little face,
No one else could take your place.

What a character you are,
Darling baby, little star,
Chubby cheeks and cheeky smile,
Into mischief all the while.

This time it's a little boy,
Such a treasure, such a joy,
My grandson means so much to me,
As I sit him on my knee,
No words describe just how I feel,
I can't believe that this is real.

Child of my son and his wife,
Since you came into my life,
I treasure every moment dear,
Every time that you are near.

Angels smiled from up above,
Sent you both for me to love,
You've blessed my life, the two of you,
Now my dreams have all come true.

Moving On

We had the urge for moving on,
The time had come for change,
Now we'd outgrown our little house,
Our lives we'd rearrange.

Our home had served its purpose,
Just like a stepping stone,
To take us on to pastures new,
A semi-rural home.

We packed our bags and boxes
And then passed on our keys,
We'd had enough of urban life,
We longed for grass and trees.

That first morning I awoke
And looked out through the glass,
The birds were singing in the trees
And pecking at the grass.

I thought back to our terraced house,
Complete with quaint back yard,
We'd found a willing buyer,
The going had been hard.

Our new garden seemed like paradise,
It filled my eyes with tears,
We'd one tree full of apples,
Another full of pears.

We had a lot of work to do,
For months we toiled away,
Bedding down at midnight,
Up at break of day.

Unknown to us a miracle –
Then formed before our eyes,
Our fruit trees blossomed year by year
To give us good supplies.

The years just flew, then came the time
For kids to fly the nest,
To seek their fortunes one by one
And give us both a rest.

But when our offspring came of age
The trees then ceased to bear,
Not one apple grew for us
And not a single pear.

Next summer as we dug the ground,
A tear came to my eye,
I realised the fruit had grown,
Until we'd said goodbye.

Never will I know just how
These things had come about,
But now I know that God makes sure
We'll never be without.

Ghosts and Graveyards

Ghostly turrets looming large,
Cobwebs overhead,
Mysterious figures scurrying past
And spectres long since dead.

A startled flurry of strange creatures,
Bats that fly at night,
Ghostly figures raining down,
Preferring little light.

A hooting owl, a full shone moon,
An eerie wail or two;
A howling wolf, a spider's web,
A graveyard's misty hue.

Advancing, he thought he heard the sound
Of a deep dark cry within;
Nearer then and nearer still
He crept a-tremblin'.

As he approached, the sound increased
And turned his blood to ice,
A creaking door, a dripping tap,
The sound of running mice.

Blood-curdling screams and piercing yells,
From pathways long and narrow;
A throbbing pain within his skull,
Shook him to his marrow.

He thought he heard a strange voice calling –
'Come with me!' it said.
With mighty yell, he swung away,
Then turned his heel and fled.

And as he sprinted on cracked paths,
Terror gripped his soul;
Our fleeing mortal disappeared –
Down a deep, dark hole.

No one knows what happened next,
His fate none ever knew;
The mystery deepened hour by hour
And year by year it grew.

Never was he seen again –
That stranger on the path,
Now night by night these tales are told,
Beside each blazing hearth.

Watch Your Step!

Hubby turned and said to me,
'Be careful what you do,
Mind your step and pay attention,
I've been watching you.

You are a trifle clumsy,
You topple frequently,
Avoid those rocky ladders
And listen carefully.

You've had burns from the oven,
And cuts from knives and such,
I'm only nagging at you
Because I care so much.

You've tripped and fallen on wet tiles
And cursed each time you fell,
You've scalded skin with turkey fat,
And had many a fainting spell.

When you've been using curling tongs
You've singed your soft white neck,
You've paper cuts and candle burns,
You'll make yourself a wreck.

Those foreign bodies in your eye
Play havoc with your tears,
You should be used to contact lenses,
You've had them for years.

Please don't leave that prop there!
Be careful where you walk,'
I said to him 'be quiet,
You're full of bloomin' talk.'

'Okay but don't come cryin'
If you have a little fall,
Please use some caution in your stride,
I've warned you after all.

Oh no! What did I tell you?
You've gone and done it now,
You've tripped and fallen twice outside,
Please, pray tell me how?'

A quick trip to the surgery
To stem that flow of blood,
'You see, you've done it once again,
Oh dear this is no good.

You'll be limping for a fortnight
Until your foot's okay,
Thank God you're here to tell the tale
And live another day!

I've wasted all my bloomin' breath
And now I've had enough,
But I'll still keep on nagging you,
And if you don't like it – tough!'

The Spot

A spot appeared upon my nose,
Just my luck! I hope it goes
Before the party at Sue and Jack's,
I thought I'd stop it in its tracks.

I bought some of that special cream,
I've heard it said 'works like a dream,'
I put it on and went to bed,
Awful thoughts ran through my head.

I tossed and turned and couldn't sleep,
Just could not resist a peep
Into the mirror at the spot,
Could not believe how big it got.

Much bigger than when I went to bed,
Very large and very red,
I put more cream upon the spot,
The more I applied, the bigger it got.

I phoned my friend who is a nurse,
'Oh, help me please, the spot's much worse.'
She came and looked and shook her head,
'You'd better get right back to bed.'

'You can't be seen with that big spot
Until it's gone down quite a lot!'
Oh deary me, I looked a freak,
And then a tear ran down my cheek.

I phoned Sue's house and told my tale,
By then I had become quite pale.
The spot was growing more and more,
Just then a knock came at the door.

'It's only me,' my mother said,
'Hurry up, get out of bed!
You will be late for work,' said she,
'I've brought you in a cup of tea.'

'What spot?' said she, as I lay crying,
'Anyone would think you're dying.'
I'd thought the spot was such a size
Then I could scarce believe my eyes,

The mirror showed no spot at all!
The 'magic' cream worked after all?
Life is never what it seems -
In absurd and silly dreams!

Decorating

I'll get up bright and early to decorate that room,
I'm full of good intentions, but first I'll need a broom,
Water, sponge and scraper, screwdriver, tools and such,
Can't wait to hang that paper, the kind I like so much.

But first there are the boring jobs, the dusty, sticky chores;
I'll strip those walls in no time, but what about the doors?
They'll need a darn good rub down, as will the skirting too,
The ceiling needs a re-paint, there's such a lot to do.

Don't forget the curtain rail, I have to take that down,
I really need a new one, which means a trip to town.
I'll need some stuff to fill the cracks, face mask to trap the dust,
That radiator needs attention, can you see that rust?

I'll order some new carpet for comfort underfoot,
And then there'll be the curtains, I'll need a lot of loot,
I'll need to gather energy, but that I cannot buy,
'Tis one thing that's essential for doing DIY.

The thought of these activities just jumbles up my brain,
I think I'll make a cup of tea and sit right down again.
The dog and I will need our walk to set our spirits free,
And later when we're back at home I'll make a cup of tea.

Now we're home I'll make that tea and sit down for a while,
I need to rest my weary legs, we've trundled many a mile.
This chair feels very comfortable, it's soft and warm and deep,
It tells me I need forty winks, my eyes are full of sleep.

Then time for lunch and after that I'll think about that stripping,
The hours have travelled quickly and I've spent too much time kipping.
I look towards the garden, those weeds I must attend,
Who's that a-knocking at the door? – oh, hello, it's my friend.

Another hour or two goes by, we've had our tea and cake,
The clock grabs my attention, some progress I must make.
Oh dear, I must prepare the dinner, hubby will be waiting,
I must postpone ideas now, of all that decorating.

While we eat we chat away about the colour schemes,
I tell him it will be a room beyond our wildest dreams.
I've washed the dishes, now I'm tired, so it's too late anyway,
I'll have an early night tonight and start another day!

Say Hello to Daddy

Say hello to daddy when you arrive;
Tell him how I wished he was alive,
When you get there ask him why he died
And bade the gate of Heaven open wide.

Ask that if he'd sat me on his knee
And told me tales of war and history,
Would it have made a difference to my world,
And would the flag of peace have been unfurled.

Ask him if he sent you here to me,
To love me and to keep me company,
And to guide me, for him, through the path of life,
And comfort me in anguish and in strife.

Tell him how he missed the joy and mirth
And the glad occasion of my birth;
Tell him of the good times we did share,
And keep him happy until I get there.

But keep from him the sorry tales of woe,
Or make believe they happened long ago;
Tell him of the giggles, fun and laughter,
Tell him we are happy ever after.

Tell him how I loved you through the years,
How we overcame the anguish and the tears,
And when in paradise we all shall meet –
I'll tell him how our lives are now complete.

I've searched a while in strange enchanted dreams
Perchance our paths would cross in starry gleams,
Alas! My soul is barred from Heaven's portal,
Until my soul has reached its time immortal.

When Your Eyes Grow Dim

When your eyes grow dim and you are past your prime,
With far more years behind you than ahead
And all your aspirations put to bed,
Be thankful you were blessed with gifts of time –

Your mirror will expose those careworn eyes
Revealing wrinkled shadows on your brow,
Forget these imperfections, and avow –
To think on sunny climes and rainbow skies.

Do not distress yourself with unfound fears,
But sweep them to a far and distant place
And pause awhile to muse on your good grace
And linger not on sorrow, pain or tears.

And when someday you've carried out your plan
And realised each dream within your mind,
'Tis then and only then at last you'll find
Contentment, fulfilment, peace of mind.